The Beginning of Forever

A Letter from One Who Was There

DECEMBER 9, 2025
GARRICK AUSTIN

Copyright © 2025 Garrick Austin

All rights reserved. No part of this book may be reproduced or transmitted in any form or by any means, electronic or mechanical, including photocopying, recording, or by any information storage and retrieval system, without permission in writing from the author and publisher.

Any resemblance to actual people, living or dead, or actual events is purely coincidental. The information contained in this book is for general information purposes only. While I endeavor to keep the information up to date and correct, I make no representations or warranties of any kind, express or implied, about the completeness, accuracy, reliability, suitability, or availability with respect to the book or the information, products, services, or any graphics contained in the book for any purpose. Any reliance you place on such information is therefore strictly at your own risk.

In no event will I be liable for any loss or damage including without limitation, indirect or consequential loss or damage, or any loss or damage whatsoever arising from loss of data or profits arising out of, or in connection with, the use of this book.

No compensation was provided for any entity, organization, enterprise or software referred to in the book.

PROLOGUE — One Who Was There

Dear Brother or Sister,

I write these words to you from a world that breathes peace in every direction—a world that has finally become what Jehovah intended when He first said, "In the beginning."[1] [2] And though the earth around us is whole now, healed and harmonious,[3] I remember clearly what it felt like when things were not this way. Not because of sorrow—Jehovah has removed that forever[4]—but because the contrast helps me appreciate the brilliance of the life we now share.

You and I did not arrive here at the same moment.
I lived through the collapse of the old world and the slow dawn of the new.
You lived your life, fell asleep in death, were resurrected during the Millennium,[5] and proved loyal in the final test.[6]

Now we stand side by side, perfected, proven, and eternal.

Back in the old system, before paradise, before resurrection, before perfection...
I was an engineer.
And if you were anything like me, your mind liked things that were:

Consistent
Reliable
Logical
Testable

Oddly enough, that's exactly what drew me to Jehovah.

When I examined the Scriptures, what reached me wasn't emotion—it was the precision of truth. The harmony of prophecy. The consistency of Jehovah's character across centuries of human history.

Truth never contradicted itself.
Jehovah never contradicted Himself.

But understanding something with the mind is not the same as letting it settle in the heart.
My heart lagged behind for many years.

Two realizations finally unlocked it for me:

1. Jehovah exists outside of time.
Time, as Genesis says, began "in the beginning."[2] Jehovah created it. Which means He is never too early, never too late—He already inhabits every moment of our lives. He heard every prayer I ever prayed before I ever prayed it.[7]

2. The life-force in us is His connection to us.
When Scripture says He is "not far from each one of us,"[8] that isn't poetry—
it's physics.
The spark that animates us comes from Him. It returns to Him when we die.[9] It sustains us every moment we live.

Of course He knows the heart.[10]
Of course He knows our thoughts.[11]
We live on the current of His life-giving power.

Now, perfected, standing with you in paradise, I understand it even more deeply.

So I write this letter not simply as history,
but as gratitude—
for Jehovah's patience,
for Christ's rule,
for the love that brought us all into forever.

The fields outside my home glow with morning light as I write.

Children laugh somewhere in the distance.
A lion stretches lazily under a fig tree.[12]
The air is thick with peace.[13]

This is the life Jehovah always intended for humanity.[14]

This is the Beginning of Forever.

And these pages will tell you how we came to stand in this dawn together.

Your brother,
who once studied truth with his mind
and now embraces it with a perfected heart

Acknowledgments

The bible, publications of The Watchtower Bible and Tract Society, Jehovah God, His son Jesus Christ, the Anointed of God, Open AI (ChatGPT) and all perfected humans.

Table of Contents

Copyright © 2025 Garrick Austin 1

PROLOGUE — One Who Was There 2

Acknowledgments 5

PART I — THE LAST DAYS OF HUMAN RULE 8

CHAPTER 1 — The Rumblings Before the End 8

CHAPTER 2 — The Fall of False Religion 10

CHAPTER 3 — "Peace and Security!" 12

CHAPTER 4 — The Final Attack on God's People ... 13

CHAPTER 5 — Armageddon and the End of Man's Governments 14

PART II — CHAPTERS 6–10 15

CHAPTER 6 — The Land Without Rulers 15

CHAPTER 7 — When the Jesus Took His Throne ... 17

CHAPTER 8 — Clearing the Earth—The First Work of Paradise 19

CHAPTER 9 — Restoring the Earth—When the Land Began to Heal 21

CHAPTER 10 — The First Resurrections on the Earth—When Death Lost Its Grip 23

PART III — CHAPTERS 11–16 26

CHAPTER 11 — Education for Eternity—When Truth Filled the Earth 26

CHAPTER 12 — Healing the Human Family—When Every Wound Began to Mend 29

CHAPTER 13 — When Paradise Began to Blossom— The Craft of a New World 32

CHAPTER 14 — The Growing Family of Man— Children Born into Peace 34

CHAPTER 15 — A Thousand Years of Peace... and Then the Shadow Returned 36

CHAPTER 16 — The Separating of Hearts—Loyalty Proven Forever 38

PART IV — CHAPTERS 17–22 + CLOSING REFLECTION 40

CHAPTER 17 — A World Without Evil—The First Breath of Forever 40

CHAPTER 18 — The Perfected Earth—Creation at Rest and in Full Bloom 42

CHAPTER 19 — The Work of Eternity—A Life of Learning, Discovery, and Joy 44

CHAPTER 20 — Echoes of the Old World—Why We Remember What Jehovah Removed 46

CHAPTER 21 — Life Without Sin—The Joy of a Perfect Heart 48

CHAPTER 22 — Forever Begins—The Dawn That Never Ends 50

CLOSING REFLECTION — A NOTE TO THE RESURRECTED ONE READING THIS 53

Dedication 55

About the Author 56

Endnotes 58

PART I — THE LAST DAYS OF HUMAN RULE

CHAPTER 1 — The Rumblings Before the End

Before the world ended, it trembled.

Not visibly at first—not with earthquakes or plagues or disasters—but with something deeper. A kind of moral fever spreading quietly across humanity. If you lived then, you remember it well:

People loved themselves more than goodness.[15]
Truth became optional.[15]
Loyalty became rare.[15]
Integrity became expensive.[15]
And peace... felt like a rumor.[16]

I remember walking through cities full of people who were empty inside.
I remember reading news that felt like prophecy written in real time.[17]
I remember watching relationships crumble, nations polarize, nature groan.[18]

Second Timothy 3:1–5[15] wasn't just a scripture—
it was the world's diagnosis.

But even then, Jehovah's people lived differently.[19]
We weren't perfect, but we were awake.
We saw the pattern.
We felt the storm building.

And even as the world unraveled, we kept preaching—
the last global warning before the final dawn.[20]

CHAPTER 2 — The Fall of False Religion

When the end finally began, it started with silence.

Not peaceful silence—
the kind that comes before a storm breaks open.

False religion—the harlot of Revelation—had sat on the nations for centuries, guiding them with lies, cloaking itself in authority.[21] But when the political powers turned on her, it happened with ruthless speed.[22]

Temples, churches, and institutions that once commanded fear found themselves abandoned.[23]
Religious leaders who claimed divine right saw their influence evaporate.

It was shocking to the world.
But not to those who knew the prophecy.

Jehovah's Witnesses weren't spared hardship—
but we were spared confusion.[24]
We knew exactly what was unfolding.
We continued our ministry with calm determination.[20]

The world didn't understand us.
But Jehovah did.
And that was enough.

CHAPTER 3 — "Peace and Security!"

Then came the strangest moment in human history.

A sudden global declaration—
a political, economic, symbolic exhale:

"Peace and Security!"[25]

I still remember hearing it on the news, the broadcasters smiling with brittle optimism. It was the final calm before the storm. A world trying to convince itself that things were improving, while prophecy whispered otherwise.

Jehovah's people understood what it meant.[26]

We didn't panic.
We didn't hide.
We held our ground and trusted the One who sees the end from the beginning.[27]

Because that declaration opened the final act of human government.

CHAPTER 4 — The Final Attack on God's People

When the world turned on Jehovah's servants,
it wasn't logical.
It wasn't political.
It was spiritual darkness rising in full force.

I remember the fear—
not the kind that chokes faith,
but the kind that makes you cling to Jehovah
with every thread of strength you have.

Governments outlawed our worship.[28]
Neighbors turned suspicious.
Authorities came with threats and force.[29]

But there was also peace.

A strange, deep, unshakeable peace—
the kind Jehovah places in the hearts of those
He intends to rescue.[30]

In those days, we saw the fulfillment of prophecy unfold not as myth,
but as reality.[31]

And then... Jehovah acted.[32]

CHAPTER 5 — Armageddon and the End of Man's Governments

When Jehovah intervened, it wasn't loud in the way humans expect.
It was decisive.

Armageddon wasn't chaos—
it was justice.[33]

Political structures collapsed like dust.[34]
Wicked systems dissolved.
The corrupt fell away like rot from a tree—
not by human violence,
but by divine removal.[35]

When the storm ended, the silence felt holy.

Survivors stepped out into a world washed clean of oppression—and I remember thinking:

The old world is gone.
Jehovah kept His promise.[36]
Now the real work begins.

PART II — CHAPTERS 6–10

CHAPTER 6 — The Land Without Rulers

The first days after Armageddon felt like stepping into a silent, unfamiliar world.
The cities that once hummed with noise were quiet.
Roads were empty.
The sky felt larger somehow, as though it had been cleared of a constant strain none of us fully noticed before.

There were no governments.[37]
No authorities.
No borders.[38]
Just human beings standing in the clean, peaceful aftermath of divine justice.

We gathered in small groups at first—family clusters, congregation friends, neighbors who had survived the storm. The absence of human rulership was startling, but it didn't bring fear.
It brought clarity.

We weren't lost.
We weren't leaderless.
We weren't without direction.

We were shepherded by Christ,[39]
guided by Jehovah,[40]

and supported by the early organization of the resurrected anointed.[41]

The world was empty of oppression, but full of possibility. And as we stood in the quiet fields and cleared streets, we felt the weight of something sacred:

We inherited a world waiting to be made new.[42]

Just as Israel once entered Canaan,[43]
we stepped into cities we did not build
and fields we did not plant—
not as conquerors,
but as caretakers of a gift.

CHAPTER 7 — When the Jesus Took His Throne

Jesus Christ's Kingdom became real to us in steady, gentle ways.

Direction came through the anointed—
not as rulers,
but as shepherds.⁴⁴
Their authority wasn't political.
It was spiritual from heaven.⁴⁵
Their spiritual presence carried no pride, only clarity.

The very first time I heard what one of the anointed spoke in the new world, I felt something settle inside me—like a compass aligning.

"There is no hurry," she said.
"There is only obedience, gratitude, and purpose."

And that became the rhythm of our early days.

We organized ourselves not around hierarchy, but around ability:

Skilled hands
Willing hearts
Steady minds

Patient teachers
Joyful laborers

There were prayers—long, quiet prayers where tears fell freely, not out of sorrow but out of relief.
The King Jesus reigned.[46]
The world was safe.
The work ahead was holy.

He didn't command by force.
He guided by love.[47]
And we followed without hesitation.

Because there is no burden in the direction of our perfect King.[48]

CHAPTER 8 — Clearing the Earth—The First Work of Paradise

The clearing of the earth was the first great labor of the new world.

We didn't rush.
We didn't destroy out of anger.
We dismantled with dignity.

Every building, every factory, every remnant of the old system was approached with reverence—not for what it represented, but for what Jehovah had replaced it with.

We examined each structure and asked:

Can it be used?
Can it be repurposed?
Should it be returned to the soil?

Useful materials became tools, homes, greenhouses, terraces.[49]
Useless or corrupt remnants returned to dust.[50]

The land responded almost immediately.

Weeds pushed through cracks as if eager for sunlight.

Birdsong returned to abandoned neighborhoods.
The wind felt clean, as though relieved.[51]

Working together deepened our love for one another:

Shared meals,
Shared prayers,
Shared sweat,
Shared silence.

Clearing the earth didn't feel like labor.
It felt like worship.

And with every piece removed, we felt closer to the paradise Jehovah envisioned.[52]

CHAPTER 9 — Restoring the Earth—When the Land Began to Heal

When the clearing ended, restoration began.

We planted the first gardens with careful hands and hopeful hearts. The soil—once tired, poisoned, overworked—welcomed the seeds like a long-lost friend.[53]

The first orchard I helped plant grew with a strength that amazed us.
Fruit swelled heavy on branches younger than logic allowed.
Rivers ran clearer each month.
Forests reclaimed hillsides.
Animals returned—calm, curious, unafraid.[54]

Homes emerged from reclaimed materials:

Wood with history,
Stone with character,
Earth with warmth.

No fences.
No locks.
No alarms.

Technology didn't vanish—
we used what was useful,
discarded what was harmful,

and kept everything in harmony.

We didn't build cities.
We built communities.

And every morning felt like Jehovah and Jesus whispering:
"Keep going. I am with you."[55]

CHAPTER 10 — The First Resurrections on the Earth—When Death Lost Its Grip

I will never forget the first resurrection.

We gathered quietly, reverently, on a soft morning glowing with gold. The air felt charged—not with fear, but with anticipation.

And then...

A figure appeared.
Human.
Whole.
Alive.[56]

They blinked into the light, breathing as if for the first time.
We approached gently.
We spoke their name softly.
Recognition dawned across their face like sunrise over still water.

In that moment, death itself felt small—
a defeated enemy with no sting left.[57]

More came.
Hundreds.
Thousands.
Millions.[58]

They returned in waves, each name restored by divine memory.[59]

People from every century,
every nation,
every background—
walking into a world where sorrow held no claim on them.[60]

Parents embraced children they had lost in the old world.
Children clung to parents they barely remembered.
Friends reunited with laughter that sounded like healing.

And teaching began:

How to read,
How to write,
How to worship,
How to live without fear.[61]

You were one of them.
One who opened their eyes into a world already healing.
One who learned, grew, loved, and later—stood firm in the final test.[62]

The resurrection proved what we had always known:

Jehovah never forgets a name.
Not one![63]

PART III — CHAPTERS 11–16

CHAPTER 11 — Education for Eternity—When Truth Filled the Earth

Once the resurrections gathered momentum and the land blossomed under Jesus Christ's rule, something extraordinary began—an education unlike anything humanity had ever known.

It didn't begin with classrooms or schedules.
It began with curiosity awakened.

People of all ages gathered in shaded fields, restored halls, and simple meeting areas. Resurrected ones from distant centuries sat beside survivors of the last days. Children who had only ever known peace sat beside adults still adjusting to a world without fear.

There were no tests.
No grades.
No competition.

Learning was not a burden—
it was joy.

We studied:

Jehovah's fulfillment of His purposes from Eden to Armageddon[64]
The life and teachings of Christ with perfect clarity[65]
The histories of nations without distortion[66]
The natural sciences as reflections of divine design[67]
The one language, music, mathematics, craftsmanship, agriculture

Everything we learned strengthened our gratitude.

I once sat beside a man resurrected from the first century. He ran his fingers across a page of Scripture and said, "I heard these words in Aramaic. Today I read them in our one language. Jehovah preserved those words for us both."[68]

Children learned with astonishing ease.
Adults learned with humility and eagerness.
The resurrected learned with wide-eyed wonder.

Each lesson felt like stepping deeper into Jehovah's mind—
and deeper into His love.

This was education without pain.
Without confusion.

Without pride.

This was learning as it was always meant to be: a pathway to true worship.[69]

CHAPTER 12 — Healing the Human Family—When Every Wound Began to Mend

Before Armageddon, humanity was held together by frayed threads—trauma, illness, fear, broken relationships. But after the resurrection and during the Thousand Years, healing swept across the human family like a gentle tide.

This healing touched every part of life.

Physical Healing

Bodies restored.[70]
Strength renewed.
Senses awakened.[71]

I watched people stand upright for the first time in decades.
I saw those once blind open their eyes to color.
I heard laughter from voices that hadn't known joy in centuries.

The resurrected arrived whole—
their bodies untouched by old injuries,
their faces calm and curious.

Emotional Healing

This healing was deeper.

People who carried scars from abuse, war, and loss no longer felt those wounds.
Old fears lost their grip.
Guilt melted away.
Grief became memory without pain.[72]

Jehovah healed not only bodies—
He healed stories.[73]

I remember a sister who said through tears, "It feels like Jehovah reached into my chest and pulled out a thorn I didn't know I still carried."

Mental Healing

No more anxiety.[74]
No more depression.
No more disordered thoughts.
No more violence born of broken minds.

Clarity filled every heart—
a clean light replacing centuries of darkness.

Healing Relationships

Families estranged for generations reunited.[75]
Resurrected children embraced parents who had mourned them.
Neighbors resolved old conflicts with ease.
Communities grew in warmth and trust.[76]

Healing became our shared language.

And it prepared us for the paradise that was beginning to rise all around us.

CHAPTER 13 — When Paradise Began to Blossom—The Craft of a New World

When the healing of humanity reached full momentum, the earth itself seemed to lean toward us with expectation.

We planted orchards and watched trees grow faster and fuller than logic allowed.[77]
We tended fields that produced food better than anything from the old world.
We restored forests and watched them come alive with animals unafraid of humans.[78]

People built homes that blended with nature:

Nestled into hills,
Perched beside rivers,
Shaded by wide trees,
Surrounded by gardens.[79]

Still, no fences.
No locks.
No alarms.
No need.

Craftsmanship flourished:

Wood carved with meaning,
Pottery shaped with joy,
Music composed without sorrow,[80]

Art born from clarity, not pain.

We reclaimed technology—
the useful, the safe, the harmonious—
and gently let go of everything born from greed,
war, or pollution.

Work wasn't toil anymore.
Work was creativity.
Work was expression.
Work was worship.[81]

Every garden
Every home
Every path
Every vineyard
Every instrument
Every crafted object

...was made with love.

Paradise wasn't built in a day—
but it blossomed steadily until every corner of
the earth sang with life.[82]

CHAPTER 14 — The Growing Family of Man—
Children Born into Peace

When the first children were born in the new world, the sound of their laughter changed everything.

These children grew up without fear.
Without sickness.
Without violence.
Without sadness.[83]

Their minds were clear from the start, unburdened by inherited trauma or inherited sin.[84]
Their hearts naturally leaned toward kindness.
Their curiosity was pure.
Their relationships were effortless.

Resurrected children, too, grew strong and joyful—
welcomed not only by their families
but by entire communities that had waited for them.

Children walked beside wolves and lions as if this had always been the way of things.[85]
They learned from elders, who told them of the world Jehovah had removed—
not to frighten them,
but to teach them gratitude.

These children became the heartbeat of the new world—
the living proof that Jehovah had restored His purpose for the human family.[86]

And you yourself knew many of them before the final test.
They were the innocence that brightened the Thousand Years.

CHAPTER 15 — A Thousand Years of Peace...
and Then the Shadow Returned

When the Thousand Years were drawing to a close, the world stood in harmony so flawless that it was easy to forget the prophecy still ahead.

Then came the moment foretold from ancient times:
Satan was released.[87]

The test did not come with armies or chaos.
It came quietly—
inside the heart.

People began to feel subtle thoughts arise:
shadows of independence,
whispers of pride,
the faint tug of self-will.

Everyone alive—resurrected or survivor—had already lived centuries of education, healing, and worship.
No one was ignorant.
No one was weak.
No one lacked opportunity.

The test was simple and absolute:

Would you choose Jehovah freely?[88]

Most did.
Including you.

Some, however, drifted.
Not dramatically.
Just truthfully.

They stepped away from Jehovah in the privacy of their own motives.⁸⁹

And when every heart had revealed itself, Jehovah removed the rebels swiftly and justly.⁹⁰

The world breathed—
lighter, cleaner, whole.

Humanity stood perfected.⁹¹
The universe quieted.
The final enemy was gone.

And eternity waited before us like an open garden.

CHAPTER 16 — The Separating of Hearts—
Loyalty Proven Forever

In the wake of the final test, a profound stillness settled over the earth.

Every person alive had chosen Jehovah—
not because of environment,
not because of pressure,
but because of love.[92]

The human family was purified.
Perfect.
Unified.[93]

You, resurrected before the test, were among those who chose Jehovah wholeheartedly when the moment came.[94]

Your loyalty is part of the fabric of eternity now. Your faith stands beside mine, and beside the faith of every perfected human who walks this earth today.

The final test didn't break humanity.
It completed it.[95]

After that day, sin disappeared from the human heart forever.
Not repressed—
removed.[96]

Every thought, every impulse, every word became pure, effortless, aligned with Jehovah's will.[97]

We stepped into a world finally ready for forever.

PART IV — CHAPTERS 17–22 + CLOSING REFLECTION

CHAPTER 17 — A World Without Evil—The First Breath of Forever

When the final test ended and the last whisper of rebellion vanished, the world felt suddenly, miraculously... light.

Not physically—
but spiritually, emotionally, atmospherically.

We stepped outside the next morning and the earth greeted us with a peace so deep it felt alive.
The sunlight seemed warmer.
The breeze carried a kind of gentle clarity.
Even the birdsong had a purity to it we had never heard before.

For the first time since Eden,
the human family was entirely loyal,
entirely united,
entirely whole.[98]

The quiet was not emptiness.
It was completeness.

I remember standing still, letting the realization wash over me:

"I will never disappoint Jehovah again."

Not because of restraint,
but because the sinful nature had been removed—
utterly, permanently, mercifully.[99]

You felt this too.
All of us did.

It was the first true breath of forever.[100]

CHAPTER 18 — The Perfected Earth—
Creation at Rest and in Full Bloom

After the test, the earth blossomed in ways we had not thought possible.

During the Thousand Years, the land healed.
After the test it perfected.[101]

Trees grew taller and fuller.
Flowers bloomed in colors we had never seen.
Animals walked the earth in unbroken peace—
lions beside oxen, wolves beside deer, children beside bears.[102]

Rivers shimmered like glass.
Oceans glowed deep blue, alive with restored coral and thriving life.
Forests whispered with the sound of wind, not danger.

Every corner of the earth felt purposeful—
crafted, tended, harmonious.

Human homes nestled into the land like part of creation:

Stones fitted by hand,
Gardens intertwined with living spaces,
Terraces overlooking rivers and orchards,
Open homes full of light and joy.[103]

Again, no fences.
No alarms.
No locked doors.

The earth was not a place to protect yourself from—
it was your inheritance.[104]

And Jehovah walked with us not through visions,
but through every detail of the perfected world.[105]

You stepped into this beauty after your resurrection,
but the fullness of perfection arrived when
you, and all of us, passed the final test.[106]

CHAPTER 19 — The Work of Eternity—A Life of Learning, Discovery, and Joy

Eternity didn't begin with a trumpet or a proclamation.
It began with possibility.

When the last trace of sin was gone, the human mind expanded.[107]
Our bodies strengthened.
Our creativity blossomed.

Every day felt like a door opening to a new horizon.

We learned without fatigue.
We created without frustration.
We explored without fear.
We worked without weariness.[108]

We studied:

Stars and galaxies,
Hidden laws of nature,
The mathematics woven into creation,
Languages from distant ages,
Music forming harmonies never heard before,
Arts and crafts shaped by perfect minds,
The history of human salvation.

We traveled the earth freely:

across mountains,
through forests,
into underwater worlds,
across continents that had been reborn.[109]

Everything revealed Jehovah's brilliance.[110]

Every discovery felt like worship.[111]

And you—
with the mind Jehovah restored to perfection—
now walk this path with all humanity,
growing endlessly,
learning endlessly,
alive endlessly.[112]

CHAPTER 20 — Echoes of the Old World— Why We Remember What Jehovah Removed

Even in this perfect world, a few gentle remnants of the old world remain—
not monuments of grief,
but markers of wisdom.

Ruins softened by vines.
Old stone stairways reclaimed by moss.
Fragments of foundations wrapped in flowers.

Children often ask:
"What were these from?"

And we answer:
"From a world that forgot Jehovah.
And from a world Jehovah removed so you could live in peace."[113]

We preserve these soft echoes not to glorify the past,
but to understand our present.

Memory no longer carries pain.[114]
Jehovah healed every scar.
But memory carries gratitude.

And the resurrected—like you—carry their stories not as burdens
but as testimonies of Jehovah's mercy.[115]

The past is no longer a shadow.
It is a teacher.

And every generation born into this paradise learns:
This world exists because Jehovah is faithful.[116]
And because humanity finally chose Him.[117]

CHAPTER 21 — Life Without Sin—The Joy of a Perfect Heart

Sin was humanity's oldest companion—
unwelcome, uninvited, and relentless.

But the day after the final test,
for the first time in all history,
sin was gone.

Not suppressed.
Not managed.
Gone.[118]

The feeling was indescribable.

Every thought was clean.
Every impulse pure.
Every desire aligned with Jehovah's will.[119]

Relationships deepened instantly:
no jealousy,
no pride,
no insecurity,
no misunderstanding.[120]

Creativity surged.
Laughter grew effortless.
Work became joy.
Worship became natural.[121]

Our hearts, once divided,
became whole.

And as you know, my friend—
because you now live this life beside us—
there is nothing sweeter,
nothing steadier,
nothing more liberating
than the constant, quiet knowledge:

We will never sin again.
Not ever.[122]

Jehovah finished His work in us.[123]
And with that, humanity truly began.

CHAPTER 22 — Forever Begins—The Dawn That Never Ends

You remember it.
I remember it.
We all do.

The first sunrise after the final test felt like creation itself was singing.

Light spread across the hills with warmth that seemed almost conscious.
The air shimmered with promise.
Animals stirred with gentle curiosity.
And every human heart pulsed with the same quiet truth:

This is the first day of eternity.[124]

Not hope.
Not prophecy.
Reality.

The Great Enemy was gone.[125]
Sin was gone.
Death was gone.[126]
Every fear was gone.

The human family—resurrected and surviving—
stood together as one perfected people.[127]

There was no sorrow.
No regret.
No doubt.

Only purpose.
Only joy.
Only forever.

That morning, I realized something profound:
Jehovah had not merely restored Eden—
He had exceeded it.[128]

We were not naive children.
We were tested, proven, and perfected adults—
ready to build, explore, learn, create, and love without end.[129]

You and I stand now in the forever He promised.[130]
This is not a dream.
This is not a metaphor.
This is the life Jehovah always intended for humanity.[131]

And as I close this letter to you, my brother or sister,
I do so with the same words that carried me through my writing:

This is not the end of the story.

Every day is the beginning of forever.

Forever awaits,
and Jehovah walks ahead.[132]

CLOSING REFLECTION — A NOTE TO THE RESURRECTED ONE READING THIS

Dear Brother or Sister,

You weren't alive to see the old-world collapse.
You probably weren't there for the early rebuilding.
But you lived the part that mattered most:

You chose Jehovah.
You passed the final test.[133]
You now stand perfected forever.[134]

This letter wasn't written to teach you...
but to welcome you.

To give you a place in the history that formed the eternity you now enjoy.
To help you see how deeply Jehovah loved humanity—
enough to heal you, test you, and perfect you.[135]

Your life is not a continuation of your old one.
Your life is a beginning.[136]

May you walk this perfect earth with wonder,
may you study creation with awe,
and may your heart remain forever loyal

to the One who gave you life twice.[137]

Welcome to forever,
my brother or sister,
my companion in eternity.

TO BE CONTINUED FOREVER

Dedication

To everyone resurrected and tested into this perfected earth—this letter is to you.

About the Author

Garrick Austin is a seasoned explorer in the ever-evolving landscape of artificial intelligence (AI). He has co-authored 2 acclaimed books on the subject: "_AI for Beginners: Unlocking the Future with Artificial Intelligence_" and "_AI for Self-Improvement: Enhancing Your Life with Artificial Intelligence_". First though using AI, he co-wrote "_Endearing Paws: The Ultimate Toy Poodle Owner's Manual_" and since the AI books he has written "_Karaoke Unleashed: Mastering the Art and Science of Sing-Along Entertainment_" and "_Echoes of the Heart Music Emotion and the Human Experience_" also with the aid of AI, further showcasing his ability to blend technology with personal passion.

Garrick then embarked on a new creative journey one that "merges photography, travel, and artificial intelligence". Those works, "_Whispering Light: My Journey Through Yosemite_" and "_Whispering Light: My Journey Through the Grand Tetons and Yellowstone_" are a deeply personal photographic explorations spanning over "50 years" of capturing the beauty of the photographer's travels. George Adams is the Photographer, Co-Author, Editor and Publisher for these.

During a time period of learning Spanish, Garrick wrote "_Spanish in Translation: Understanding the Heart of the Language: 2,000 Spanish Expressions Decoded: A Journey into Language and Meaning_".

Garrick's unique perspectives stem from a rich background in military service, technological innovation, pursuit of spiritual truths and lifelong learning. His military and technical training in analog and digital electronics laid the groundwork for a successful career in electronics and computer systems engineering. Success brought early retirement affording him the time & opportunity to pursue his passions—photography, artificial intelligence, music and most recently contemplation of what the future holds for us all in his latest book, *"The Beginning of Forever-A Letter from One Who Was There"*.

Throughout his journey, Garrick has remained dedicated to understanding and harnessing AI to empower others. His work spans diverse domains, from crafting personalized learning experiences and advancing health and well-being, to enhancing creative outlets such as photography, music, and writing.

Garrick Austin's dedication to innovation, learning, and sharing knowledge is evident in his work, making him a trusted guide for those eager to explore the intersections of technology, creativity, and personal growth.
garrickaustin60@gmail.com

Endnotes

New World Translation of the Holy Scriptures (Study Edition)
https://www.jw.org/en/library/bible/study-bible/books/

[1] Isaiah 42:9 — Jehovah foretells new things before they appear.

[2] Genesis 1:1 — "In the beginning God created the heavens and the earth."

[3] Psalm 37:29; Isaiah 65:21–25 — Earth restored; righteous dwell securely.

[4] Revelation 21:4 — Death, pain, and sorrow removed forever.

[5] John 5:28–29; Acts 24:15; Revelation 20:12–13 — Resurrection during Christ's Millennial Reign.

[6] Revelation 20:7–10 — Final test after the thousand years.

[7] Psalm 139:4; Matthew 6:8 — Jehovah knows our words and needs before we speak.

[8] Acts 17:27–28 — "He is not far from each one of us... in him we have life."

[9] Ecclesiastes 12:7 — "The spirit returns to the true God who gave it."

[10] 1 Samuel 16:7 — Jehovah sees what the heart is.

[11] Hebrews 4:13 — All things are naked and exposed to His sight.

[12] Isaiah 11:6–9 — Peace between humans and formerly dangerous animals.

[13] Psalm 72:7; Isaiah 32:17–18 — Abundant peace; secure dwelling.

[14] Genesis 1:28; Psalm 37:29 — Jehovah's original purpose for humankind.

[15] 2 Timothy 3:1–5 — Moral decay in "the last days."

[16] Luke 21:25–26 — Anxiety, fear, and distress grip the nations.

[17] Matthew 24:7–14 — Global troubles and preaching work develop as prophecy unfolds.

[18] Romans 8:19–22 — Creation "groans" under corruption.

[19] Isaiah 43:10–12 — Jehovah's people serve as His witnesses.

²⁰ Matthew 24:14 — The good news preached worldwide before the end.
²¹ Revelation 17:1–5 — Babylon the Great misleads the nations.
²² Revelation 17:16–17 — Political powers destroy the harlot.
²³ Revelation 18:2–8 — Babylon the Great collapses suddenly.
²⁴ 1 Thessalonians 5:4–5 — God's people are not caught unawares.
²⁵ 1 Thessalonians 5:3 — "Peace and security!" signals sudden destruction.
²⁶ Matthew 24:42–44 — Christ's followers stay awake and watchful.
²⁷ Isaiah 46:10 — Jehovah declares the end from the beginning.
²⁸ Amos 8:11–12; Matthew 10:22 — True worship suppressed; hatred of God's servants.
²⁹ Luke 21:12, 17 — Followers of Christ persecuted and hated.
³⁰ Isaiah 26:3 — Perfect peace given to those trusting in Jehovah.
³¹ John 16:2; Matthew 24:9 — Prophecies fulfilled regarding opposition.
³² Ezekiel 38:18–23 — Jehovah intervenes to save His people.
³³ Revelation 16:14, 16 — Nations gathered to Armageddon.
³⁴ Daniel 2:44 — God's Kingdom crushes human governments.
³⁵ Revelation 19:11–21 — Christ executes judgment on the wicked.
³⁶ Psalm 37:10–11; Proverbs 2:21–22 — The wicked removed; the meek remain.
³⁷ Hosea 3:4–5 — Without human rulers.
³⁸ Micah 4:3–4 — Nations no longer fight; true peace.
³⁹ Revelation 20:4, 6 — Christ and the anointed rule spiritually.
⁴⁰ Isaiah 33:22 — Jehovah is King, Judge, and Lawgiver.
⁴¹ 1 Corinthians 6:2 — The anointed serve in judging roles.

[42] Revelation 21:5 — "I am making all things new."
[43] Deuteronomy 6:10–11 — Inheritance of cities not built by themselves.
[44] Matthew 19:28; Revelation 20:6 — The anointed shepherd God's people.
[45] Revelation 11:15 — The Kingdom of Christ established.
[46] Psalm 72:1–7 — Peaceful, righteous rule of the Messianic King.
[47] Matthew 11:28–30 — Christ's leadership is gentle and loving.
[48] Psalm 2:6–12 — Blessings for those taking refuge in Jehovah's King.
[49] Isaiah 65:21–22 — Building and planting in peace.
[50] Ezekiel 36:33–35 — Ruins restored; land becomes like Eden.
[51] Psalm 104:30 — Jehovah renews the face of the earth.
[52] Isaiah 35:1–2, 7 — Earth blossoms under divine blessing.
[53] Psalm 67:6 — "The earth will give its produce."
[54] Isaiah 11:6–9 — Peace among animals and humans.
[55] Isaiah 41:10; 43:2 — Jehovah assures His people of His presence.
[56] John 5:28–29 — "All in the memorial tombs... will come out."
[57] 1 Corinthians 15:26, 55–57 — Death brought to nothing.
[58] Revelation 20:12–13 — The dead raised "great and small."
[59] Luke 20:37–38 — "All live to Him"; Jehovah remembers each person.
[60] Revelation 21:4 — Sorrow and crying are gone.
[61] Isaiah 54:13 — "All your children will be taught by Jehovah."
[62] Revelation 20:7–10 — Final test after the thousand years.
[63] Isaiah 49:15–16 — Jehovah never forgets even one of His people.
[64] Isaiah 55:11 — Jehovah's purposes never fail.
[65] John 17:3 — Knowledge of Christ leads to eternal life.
[66] Psalm 98:1–3; Daniel 2:20–22 — Jehovah reveals truth and removes distortion.
[67] Psalm 19:1–4 — Creation reveals Jehovah's design.
[68] Isaiah 40:8 — Jehovah preserves His word.

⁶⁹ Jeremiah 31:33–34 — All will know Jehovah.
⁷⁰ Isaiah 35:5–6 — Blind see, lame leap.
⁷¹ Revelation 21:4 — No pain or suffering.
⁷² Isaiah 65:17 — Former pains not remembered.
⁷³ Psalm 147:3 — Jehovah heals the brokenhearted.
⁷⁴ Philippians 4:7 — Peace of God guards hearts and minds.
⁷⁵ Malachi 4:6 — Family hearts reconciled.
⁷⁶ Colossians 3:12–14 — Love brings unity.
⁷⁷ Amos 9:13–14 — Land produces abundantly.
⁷⁸ Isaiah 11:6–9 — Restored harmony with animals.
⁷⁹ Isaiah 65:21–22 — Peaceful homebuilding.
⁸⁰ Psalm 98:4–6 — Joyful worship in music.
⁸¹ Psalm 104:24–28 — Work reflects Jehovah's wisdom.
⁸² Psalm 72:16; Isaiah 35:1–2 — Earth blossoms richly.
⁸³ Revelation 21:4 — No more tears, pain, or death.
⁸⁴ Romans 8:21 — Creation freed from corruption.
⁸⁵ Isaiah 11:6–9 — Children safe with animals.
⁸⁶ Genesis 1:28; Psalm 37:29 — Jehovah's purpose for families restored.
⁸⁷ Revelation 20:7–10 — Satan released for final test.
⁸⁸ Deuteronomy 30:19 — Choose life by choosing Jehovah.
⁸⁹ James 1:14–15 — Desire tests motives.
⁹⁰ Revelation 20:9 — Jehovah destroys final rebels.
⁹¹ 1 Peter 5:10 — Jehovah makes His people firm and stable.
⁹² Deuteronomy 10:12 — Obedience motivated by love.
⁹³ Malachi 3:17–18 — Distinction between righteous and wicked.
⁹⁴ Revelation 20:4 — Loyal ones rewarded with life.
⁹⁵ James 1:12 — Crown of life for those who endure.
⁹⁶ Romans 6:7 — Sin fully removed after final test.
⁹⁷ Jeremiah 31:33 — God's law written on perfected hearts.
⁹⁸ Zephaniah 3:9 — All serve Jehovah with one accord.
⁹⁹ Romans 8:21 — Freedom from corruption.
¹⁰⁰ Isaiah 35:10 — Everlasting joy.
¹⁰¹ Revelation 21:5 — Jehovah makes all things new.
¹⁰² Isaiah 11:6–9 — Complete peace in creation.
¹⁰³ Isaiah 65:21–22 — Secure, satisfying homes.
¹⁰⁴ Psalm 37:29 — Earth inherited forever.
¹⁰⁵ Revelation 21:3 — God resides with mankind.

[106] Isaiah 35:1–7 — Earth perfect after deliverance.
[107] Isaiah 11:9 — Knowledge of Jehovah fills the earth.
[108] Isaiah 40:31 — Strength renewed without weariness.
[109] Psalm 72:8; Micah 4:4 — Peaceful dominion and freedom.
[110] Psalm 19:1 — Heavens declare God's glory.
[111] Psalm 111:2 — Jehovah's works studied and delighted in.
[112] Ecclesiastes 3:11 — Eternity placed in human hearts.
[113] 2 Peter 3:7, 13 — Old world removed; new world of righteousness.
[114] Isaiah 65:17 — Former troubles no longer remembered with pain.
[115] Psalm 103:11–12 — Jehovah's mercy removes sins far away.
[116] Psalm 119:90 — Jehovah's faithfulness endures.
[117] Deuteronomy 30:19–20 — Choosing Jehovah leads to life.
[118] Romans 6:7 — Freed from sin completely.
[119] Jeremiah 31:33 — Law written on hearts.
[120] Zephaniah 3:13 — No lies, no injustice.
[121] Psalm 100:2; 40:8 — Joyful service; delight in Jehovah's will.
[122] Revelation 20:10 — Devil destroyed forever.
[123] Philippians 1:6 — Jehovah completes His work.
[124] Isaiah 60:19–20 — Everlasting light; no gloom.
[125] Revelation 20:10 — Satan permanently destroyed.
[126] Revelation 21:4 — Death no more.
[127] Zephaniah 3:9 — Unified worship.
[128] Ephesians 3:20 — Jehovah exceeds all expectations.
[129] 1 Corinthians 2:9 — Things prepared beyond imagination.
[130] Psalm 37:29 — Everlasting life on earth.
[131] Genesis 1:28; Isaiah 45:18 — Earth created to be inhabited.
[132] Isaiah 30:21 — Jehovah guides His people.
[133] Revelation 20:7–10 — Final test passed.
[134] Revelation 21:3–4 — Perfected forever.
[135] James 1:12 — Crown of life.

[136] Isaiah 65:17 — New beginning; former troubles forgotten.
[137] John 11:25; Acts 17:31 — Life through resurrection and righteous judgment.

Made in the USA
Coppell, TX
09 January 2026